Introduction

It's easy to save treasured recipes with this handy recipe binder from the Pillsbury Kitchens. You choose the way to organize them—arrange by familiar categories such as soups, salads, main dishes, desserts or appetizers—organize in alphabetical order—or sort by the original source of the recipe. Whatever method you use, the binder will allow you to keep favorite recipes neat, all in one place, and easily retrieve them when necessary.

Also included in the binder are helpful hints and tips on a variety of subjects to help you in the kitchen. There's a great glossary of cooking procedures, information on food safety and helpful tips on types of cheeses, plus much more. We know you will be delighted with your new recipe binder and find it useful every time you cook!

Cooking Terms Glossary

AL DENTE: Description for the doneness of pasta cooked until tender but firm to the bite.

BASTE: Spoon liquid over food (pan juices over turkey) during cooking to keep it moist.

BLANCH: Plunge food into boiling water for a brief time to preserve color, texture and nutritional value or to remove the skin (vegetables, fruits, nuts).

BREAD: Coat a food (fish, meat, vegetables) by dipping into a liquid (beaten egg or milk), then into bread crumbs, cracker crumbs or cornmeal before frying or baking.

BROIL: Cook directly under a red-hot heating unit.

BROWN: Cook quickly over high heat, causing the surface of the food to turn brown.

CHOP: Cut food into coarse or fine irregular-shaped pieces, using a knife, food chopper, blender or food processor.

CRISP-TENDER: Description of doneness for vegetables cooked so they retain some of their crisp texture.

CRUSH: Press into very fine particles; for example, crushing a clove of garlic with a chef's knife or garlic press.

CUBE: Cut food into squares $\frac{1}{2}$ inch or larger, using a knife.

DASH: Less than $\frac{1}{8}$ teaspoon of an ingredient.

DEGLAZE: After panfrying a food, remove excess fat from the skillet, then add a small amount of liquid (broth, water, wine) and stir to loosen browned bits of food in the skillet. This mixture is used as a base for sauce.

DICE: Cut food into squares smaller than $\frac{1}{2}$ inch, using a knife.

FLUTE: Pinching pastry with your fingers to make a finished, decorative edge.

FRY: Cook in hot fat over moderate or high heat. See also Panbroil, Panfry, Sauté.

GLAZE: Brush, spread or drizzle an ingredient (meat stock, jam, melted chocolate) on hot or cold food to give it a glossy appearance or hard finish.

GRATE: Rub a hard-textured food (chocolate, citrus peel, Parmesan cheese) against the small, rough, sharp-edged holes of a grater to reduce it to tiny particles. When grating citrus peel, be sure to grate only the outer skin, not the bitter white inner membrane.

GREASE: Rub the bottom and sides of a pan with shortening, using pastry brush, waxed paper or paper towel. Or spray with cooking spray. Grease pans to prevent food from sticking during baking (muffins, some casseroles). Don't use butter or margarine for greasing, unless specified in a recipe, because they usually contain salt that may cause hot foods to stick.

GREASE AND FLOUR: After greasing a pan with shortening, sprinkle it with small amount of flour and shake the pan to distribute it evenly. Then, turn the pan upside down and tap the bottom to remove excess flour. Grease and flour pans to prevent sticking during baking.

HULL: Remove the stem and leaves with a knife or huller (strawberries).

JULIENNE: Cut into thin, matchlike strips with a knife or food processor (fruits, vegetables, meats).

KNEAD: Work dough on a floured surface into a smooth, elastic mass, using your hands or an electric mixer with dough hooks. Kneading develops the gluten in flour and gives an even texture and a smooth, rounded top.

MARINATE: Let food stand in a marinade—a savory, acidic liquid—in a glass or plastic container for several hours to add flavor or to tenderize. Always refrigerate marinating foods.

MINCE: Cut food into very fine pieces—smaller than chopped, but bigger than crushed—with a knife.

PANBROIL: Cook meat or other food quickly in an ungreased or lightly greased skillet.

PANFRY: Fry meat or other food in a skillet, using varying amounts of fat and usually pouring off the fat from the meat during cooking. See also Fry, Panbroil, Sauté.

POACH: Cook in simmering liquid just below the boiling point (eggs, fish).

POUND: Flatten boneless cuts of chicken and meat, using a meat mallet or the flat side of a meat pounder, until they're a uniform thickness.

PUREE: Blend food until it's smooth, using a blender or food processor.

REDUCE: Boil liquid, uncovered, to evaporate some of the liquid and intensify the flavor of the remaining liquid.

SAUTÉ: Cook over medium-high heat in a small amount of fat, using a frequent tossing or turning motion. See also Fry, Panbroil, Panfry.

SCALD: Heat liquid to just below the boiling point and tiny bubbles form at the edge. A thin skin will form on the top of scalded milk.

SCORE: Lightly cutting the surface of a food about $\frac{1}{4}$ inch deep, using a knife. Scoring helps cooking and flavoring or it may be used for appearance (meat, yeast bread).

SEAR: Brown meat quickly over high heat.

SHRED: Cut into long, thin pieces using the round, smooth holes of a shredder, a knife or food processor.

SIMMER: Cook in liquid on the stove top just below the boiling point while bubbles rise slowly and break just below the surface. Simmering usually is done after reducing heat from a boil.

SKIM: Remove the top layer of fat or foam that floats on top from a soup or broth, using a spoon, ladle or skimmer (a flat utensil with holes in it).

SOFT PEAKS: Egg whites or whipping cream beaten until the moist, glossy peaks are rounded or curl when you lift the beaters from the bowl. See also Stiff Peaks.

STEAM: Cook food by placing it on a rack or in a special steamer basket over a small amount of boiling water in a covered pan.

STEW: Cook slowly in a small amount of liquid for a long time (stewed fruit, beef stew).

STIFF PEAKS: Egg whites or whipping cream beaten until moist, glossy peaks stand up straight when you lift the beaters from the bowl. See also Soft Peaks.

STIR-FRY: A Chinese method of quickly cooking similar-size pieces of food in a small amount of hot oil over high heat, lifting and stirring constantly with a turner or large spoon.

STRAIN: Pour a mixture or liquid through a fine sieve or strainer to remove larger particles.

ZEST: The outside colored layer of citrus fruit (oranges, lemons) that contains aromatic oils and flavor. It also means to remove the outside layer of citrus fruit in fine strips, using a knife, citrus zester or vegetable peeler.

Mixing Terms

BEAT: Combine ingredients vigorously with a spoon, fork, wire whisk, hand beater or electric mixer until smooth.

BLEND: Combine ingredients with a spoon, wire whisk or rubber scraper until very smooth, or to combine ingredients in a blender or food processor.

CUT IN: Thoroughly combine butter, margarine or shortening with dry ingredients. As you cut in the fat, it will begin to clump with the dry ingredients. Use a pastry blender with an up-and-down rocking motion until the particles are the desired size, such as the size of a pea. Or cut in by crisscrossing two knives or using the side of a table fork.

FOLD: Lightly combine ingredients without removing air. With a rubber spatula, cut down vertically through the mixture. Next, slide the spatula across the bottom of the bowl and up the side, turning the mixture over. Continue this down-across-up-over motion while rotating the bowl $\frac{1}{4}$ turn with each series of strokes.

WHIP: Beat ingredients to add air and increase volume until light and fluffy (cream, egg whites).

Yields and Equivalents

Bacon	½ cup crumbled	8 slices, crisply cooked
Bananas	1 cup sliced 1 cup mashed	1 medium or 2 small 2 medium
Beans, dried	5 to 6 cups cooked	1 pound dried (2¼ cups)
Beans, green or wax	3 cups 1-inch pieces	1 pound
Bread, white	1 cup soft crumbs 1 cup dry crumbs	1½ slices 4 to 5 slices, oven-dried
Broccoli, fresh	2 cups flowerets, 1-inch pieces or chopped	6 ounces
Carrots	1 cup shredded 1 cup ¼-inch slices	1½ medium 2 medium
Cauliflower	3 cups flowerets	1 pound
Chocolate Chips	1 cup	6 ounces
Unsweetened or semisweet baking	1 square or bar	1 ounce
Crumbs, finely crushed Chocolate wafer Graham cracker Saltine cracker Vanilla wafer	1½ cups 1½ cups 1 cup 1½ cups	27 cookies 21 squares 29 squares 38 cookies
Eggplant	1 medium 2 cups ½-inch pieces	1½ pounds 12 ounces
Eggs, large Whole	1 cup 1 egg	4 large eggs ¼ cup fat-free cholesterol-free egg product
Whites	1 cup	7 to 8 large eggs (use only meringue powder or dried egg whites for favorite recipes that call for raw egg whites—both products are pasteurized)
Yolks	1 cup	8 or 9 large eggs
Garlic	½ teaspoon finely chopped	1 medium clove
Lemons or limes	1½ to 3 teaspoons grated peel 2 to 3 tablespoons juice	1 medium 1 medium

Lettuce

Iceberg or romaine
	1 medium head	1½ pounds
	2 cups shredded	5 ounces
	6 cups bite-size pieces	1 pound

Meat, cooked

Beef, pork or poultry
	1 cup chopped or bite-size pieces	6 ounces

Mushrooms, fresh

	6 cups sliced	1 pound
	2½ cups chopped	8 ounces

Nuts, without shells

Chopped	1 cup	4 ounces
Whole or halves	3 to 4 cups	1 pound

Onions

Green, with tops	2 tablespoons chopped	2 medium
	¼ cup sliced	4 medium
Yellow or white	½ cup chopped	1 medium

Oranges

	1 to 2 tablespoons grated peel	1 medium
	⅓ to ½ cup juice	1 medium

Pasta, macaroni, egg noodles or spaghetti

	4 cups cooked	6 to 8 ounces uncooked (dried)

Peaches or pears

	2 cups sliced	3 medium (1 pound)

Peppers, bell

	½ cup chopped	1 small
	1 cup chopped	1 medium

Potatoes

New	10 to 12 small	1½ pounds
Red, white, sweet or yams	1 medium	5 to 6 ounces
Red or white	1 cup ½-inch pieces	1 medium

Rice, regular long grain

	3 cups cooked	1 cup uncooked

Shrimp

(uncooked, with shells)
Jumbo	1 pound	21 to 25 count
Large	1 pound	31 to 35 count
Medium	1 pound	41 to 45 count
Small	1 pound	51 to 60 count

Shrimp
(cooked, without shells)
	1 pound	1⅓ pounds uncooked, with shells

Squash

Summer: Crookneck (yellow) or zucchini	2 cups ¼-inch slices, chopped or shredded	1 medium
Winter: Acorn, buttercup, butternut or spaghetti	1 medium	1½ to 2½ pounds

Tomatoes

	1 cup chopped	1 large

Emergency Substitutions

Using the ingredients recommended in a recipe is best. But if you have to substitute, try the following:

INSTEAD OF	AMOUNT	USE
Baking powder	1 teaspoon	$\frac{1}{4}$ teaspoon baking soda plus $\frac{1}{2}$ teaspoon cream of tartar
Bread crumbs, dry	$\frac{1}{4}$ cup	$\frac{1}{4}$ cup finely crushed cracker crumbs, corn flakes or quick-cooking or old-fashioned oats
Broth, chicken, beef or vegetable	1 cup	1 teaspoon chicken, beef or vegetable bouillon granules (or 1 cube) dissolved in 1 cup boiling water
Brown sugar, packed	1 cup	1 cup granulated sugar plus 2 tablespoons molasses or dark corn syrup
Buttermilk or sour milk	1 cup	1 tablespoon lemon juice or white vinegar plus enough milk to make 1 cup; let stand a few minutes. Or 1 cup plain yogurt.
Chocolate		
Semisweet baking	1 ounce	1 ounce unsweetened baking chocolate plus 1 tablespoon sugar
Semisweet chips	1 cup	6 ounces semisweet baking chocolate, chopped
Unsweetened baking	1 ounce	3 tablespoons baking cocoa plus 1 tablespoon shortening or margarine
Corn syrup		
Light	1 cup	1 cup sugar plus $\frac{1}{4}$ cup water
Dark	1 cup	1 cup light corn syrup; $\frac{3}{4}$ cup light corn syrup plus $\frac{1}{4}$ cup molasses; or 1 cup maple-flavored syrup
Cornstarch	1 tablespoon	2 tablespoons all-purpose flour or 4 teaspoons quick-cooking tapioca

INSTEAD OF	AMOUNT	USE
Eggs	1 large	2 egg whites; $\frac{1}{4}$ cup fat-free cholesterol-free egg product; 2 egg yolks (for custards or puddings); or 2 egg yolks plus 1 tablespoon water (for cookies or bars)
Fats, solid	Any amount	Butter, margarine, lard, shortening, vegetable oil or spread with at least 65 percent fat.
Flour		
All-purpose	1 cup	1 cup plus 2 tablespoons cake flour
Cake	1 cup	1 cup minus 2 tablespoons all-purpose flour
Self-rising	1 cup	1 cup all-purpose flour plus $1\frac{1}{2}$ teaspoons baking powder and $\frac{1}{2}$ teaspoon salt
Garlic, finely chopped	1 medium clove	$\frac{1}{8}$ teaspoon garlic powder or $\frac{1}{4}$ teaspoon instant minced garlic
Herbs, chopped fresh	1 tablespoon	$\frac{3}{4}$ to 1 teaspoon dried herbs
Honey	1 cup	$1\frac{1}{4}$ cups sugar plus $\frac{1}{4}$ cup water or apple juice
Milk, regular or low-fat	1 cup	$\frac{1}{2}$ cup evaporated milk plus $\frac{1}{2}$ cup water; or nonfat dry milk prepared as directed on package
Mustard, yellow	1 tablespoon	1 teaspoon ground mustard
Poultry seasoning	1 teaspoon	$\frac{1}{4}$ teaspoon ground thyme plus $\frac{3}{4}$ teaspoon ground sage
Pumpkin or apple pie spice	1 teaspoon	Mix $\frac{1}{2}$ teaspoon ground cinnamon, $\frac{1}{4}$ teaspoon ground ginger, $\frac{1}{8}$ teaspoon ground allspice and $\frac{1}{8}$ teaspoon ground nutmeg.
Tomato juice	1 cup	$\frac{1}{2}$ cup tomato sauce plus $\frac{1}{2}$ cup water
Tomato paste	$\frac{1}{2}$ cup	1 cup tomato sauce cooked uncovered until reduced to $\frac{1}{2}$ cup
Tomato sauce	2 cups	$\frac{3}{4}$ cup tomato paste plus 1 cup water
Yogurt, plain	1 cup	1 cup sour cream

Recommended Meat Doneness

Meat	Thermometer Reading After Cooking	Color of Cooked Meat When Small Cut is Made
Beef		
Roasts	140°F. (for medium-rare)*	Does not apply
	155°F. (for medium)*	Does not apply
Other Beef Cuts	145°F. (medium-rare)	Very pink in center and slightly brown toward exterior
	160°F. (medium)	Light pink in center and brown toward exterior
Ground Beef	170°F. (well)	No longer pink in center and juices run clear
Loaves	160°F. (medium)	Does not apply
Patties	160°F. (medium)	No longer pink in center and juices run clear
Veal		
Roasts	155°F. (for medium)*	Does not apply
Other Veal Cuts	160°F. (medium)	Slightly pink in center
Pork		
Roasts	155°F. (for medium)*	Does not apply
	165°F. (for well)*	Does not apply
Other Pork Cuts	160°F. (medium)	No longer pink in center
	170°F. (well)	No longer pink in center
Ground Pork	170°F. (well)	No longer pink in center
Ham, fully cooked	135°F.*	Heated through
Lamb		
Roasts	140°F. (for medium-rare)*	Does not apply
	155°F. (for medium)*	Does not apply
Other Lamb Cuts	145°F. (medium-rare)	Pink in center
	160°F. (medium)	Light pink in center

*Roasts and hams will continue to cook after being removed from oven, so the temperature will rise about 5°F. Pork should reach a final temperature (after standing) at 160°F.

Timetable for Roasting Poultry

Ready-to-Cook Weight (pounds)	Oven Temperature	Approximate Roasting Time* (hours)
Whole Chicken (stuffed)		
3 to 3½	325°F.	2 to 2½
Whole Chicken (not stuffed)		
3 to 3½	375°F.	1¾ to 2
Duck		
3½ to 4	350°F.	2
5 to 5½	350°F.	3
Goose		
7 to 9	350°F.	2½ to 3
9 to 11	350°F.	3 to 3½
11 to 13	350°F.	3½ to 4
Pheasant		
2 to 3	350°F.	1¼ to 1½
Rock Cornish Hen		
1 to 1½	350°F.	1 to 1¼
Whole Turkey (stuffed)		
8 to 12	325°F.	3 to 3½
12 to 14	325°F.	3½ to 4
14 to 18	325°F.	4 to 4¼
18 to 20	325°F.	4¼ to 4¾
20 to 24	325°F.	4¾ to 5¼
Whole Turkey (not stuffed)		
8 to 12	325°F.	2¾ to 3
12 to 14	325°F.	3 to 3¾
14 to 18	325°F.	3¾ to 4¼
18 to 20	325°F.	4¼ to 4½
20 to 24	325°F.	4½ to 5
Turkey Breast (bone-in)		
2 to 4	325°F.	1½ to 2
3 to 5	325°F.	1½ to 2½
5 to 7	325°F.	2 to 2½

*Times given are for unstuffed birds unless noted. Stuffed birds other than turkey require 15 to 30 minutes longer. Begin checking turkey doneness about 1 hour before end of recommended roasting time. For prestuffed turkeys purchased at your grocer or meat market, follow package directions very carefully—do not use this timetable.

Timetable for Broiling or Grilling Poultry

Poultry Type	Approximate Weight (pounds)	Approximate Broiling Time	Approximate Grilling Time	Doneness
Chicken				
Cut-up chicken pieces	3 to 3½	Skin sides down 30 minutes; turn. Broil 15 to 25 minutes longer (7 to 9 inches from heat)	35 to 40 minutes (dark meat may take longer to cook)	Cook until juice of chicken is no longer pink when centers of thickest pieces are cut.
Breast halves (bone-in)	2½ to 3	25 to 35 minutes (7 to 9 inches from heat)	20 to 25 minutes	Cook until juice of chicken is no longer pink when centers of thickest pieces are cut.
Breast halves (boneless)	1¼	15 to 20 minutes, turning once (4 to 6 inches from heat)	15 to 20 minutes	Cook until juice of chicken is no longer pink when centers of thickest pieces are cut.
Wings	3 to 3½	10 minutes, turning once (5 to 7 inches from heat)	12 to 18 minutes	Cook until juice of chicken is no longer pink when centers of thickest pieces are cut.
Ground turkey or chicken patties (½ inch thick)	1	6 minutes on each side (3 inches from heat)	15 to 20 minutes	Cook until no longer pink in center.
Turkey				
Tenderloins	1 to 1½	8 to 12 minutes on each side (6 inches from heat)	20 to 30 minutes	Cook until juice of turkey is no longer pink when centers of thickest pieces are cut.
Breast slices	1 to 1½	7 minutes, turning once (4 inches from heat)	8 to 10 minutes	Cook until turkey is no longer pink in center.
Rock Cornish Hens*	2 to 3 (two hens)	30 to 40 minutes (4 to 6 inches from heat)	30 to 40 minutes	Cook until meat thermometer reads 180°F. and juice of hen is no longer pink when center of thigh is cut.

Cut hens in half before broiling or grilling for best results.

Cooking with Herbs

A pinch of dried herbs or a snippet of fresh herbs adds oomph to just about any food, from iced tea to tomatoes. Some herbs grow wild and some are cultivated on herb farms, but you can easily grow kitchen favorites such as basil, parsley, oregano and chives in your garden or in windowsill pots. Keep your kitchen scissors handy to snip herbs for a simple but impressive garnish.

Herbs range in flavor from delicate and sweet to strong and savory. Sometimes just a little bit goes a long way, especially with the more bold herbs such as rosemary and oregano. If you're using an herb for the first time, start out with 1 teaspoon of fresh herb or $\frac{1}{4}$ teaspoon of dried herb for every four servings. Taste, then add more—a little at a time—until the flavor's just right.

After measuring dried herbs, crumble them in your hand to release their flavor before adding to your recipe. Use a kitchen scissors or knife to cut fresh herbs. Because their flavor isn't as concentrated, you'll need three to four times more fresh herbs than dried.

Cooking with herbs is an adventure with exciting flavor combinations and uses for you to discover.

Cooking with Spices and Seeds

Centuries ago, spices were the treasures of kings, as much cherished and sought after as gold. Today, you don't have to sail the Seven Seas to find them—they're available at your supermarket. What are spices, exactly? Most consist of the seeds, shells, buds, fruit or flower parts, bark or roots of plants that grow in the tropical regions of the world.

If you want to crush or blend the seeds of spices, use a mortar and pestle, spice grinder or small electric grinder. Some cooks like to toast spices and seeds because toasting intensifies the flavor. Spices that are good for toasting include cumin, coriander, fennel seed, cardamom, cloves, cinnamon sticks and mustard seed. To toast, spread a thin layer of spice or seed in an ungreased skillet, and shake or stir over low heat. Watch so they don't burn! When the aroma really strengthens, take the skillet off the heat and pour out the spice or seed. Let it cool, then store in a container with a tight-fitting lid.

Storing Seasonings

To store most fresh herbs, wrap the stems in a damp paper towel, then put the herbs in a plastic bag and refrigerate.

Keep herbs such as parsley and cilantro fresh in a little "vase" in the refrigerator. Cut about $\frac{1}{8}$ to $\frac{1}{4}$ inch off the bottoms of stems so the water can be absorbed into the herb. Fill a jar with about two inches of water, place the stems in the water, then put a plastic bag over the herbs. Hold the bag in place with a rubber band around the neck of the jar. Most herbs will keep 1 to 2 weeks.

That spice rack hanging next to the stove may look homey, but being close to heat is tough on spices, dried herbs and seeds. Instead, store them in airtight containers away from heat, light and moisture but still within easy reach of where you'll be cooking. Dried herbs, spices and seasonings can be stored 1 to 2 years, although over time, the flavor may become weaker. Paprika, red pepper (cayenne) and chili powder should be refrigerated to retain color and guard against infestation. This is particularly important during the summer months and in hot climates.

After opening marinades, store them in the refrigerator.

Herb Chart

HERB AND FORM	FLAVOR	USE
Basil (fresh and dried leaves, ground)	Sweet and spicy; a cross between cloves and black licorice; reminiscent of pesto	Eggs, meats, pesto, salads, soups, stews, tomato dishes
Bay leaves (dried leaves)	Earthy, grassy, slightly piney; reminiscent of beef stew	Meats, pickling, sauces, soups, stews, vegetables
Chives (fresh, freeze-dried)	Tastes like mild green onions	Appetizers, cream soups, eggs, garnish, salads
Cilantro (fresh; also called Chinese parsley)	Slightly soapy; reminiscent of pico de gallo (salsa)	Chinese, Italian and Mexican dishes, garnish, pasta salads, pesto
Dill weed (fresh, dried)	Fresh, peppery and tangy; tastes like dill pickles	Breads, cheese, fish, salads, sauces, vegetables
Lemongrass (fresh)	Sour lemon flavor	Soups, tea, Thai dishes
Marjoram (fresh and dried leaves, ground)	Mild, slightly woodsy and flowery; reminiscent of spaghetti sauce	Cottage cheese, fish, lamb, poultry, sausages, soups, stews, stuffings, vegetables
Mint (fresh, dried)	Strong, cool, fresh, sweet; reminiscent of after-dinner mints	Beverages, desserts, fish, lamb, sauces, soups
Oregano (fresh and dried leaves, ground)	Stronger than marjoram, slightly bitter; reminiscent of pizza	Cheese, eggs, fish, Italian dishes, meats, sauces, soups, vegetables
Parsley (fresh curly leaf, fresh Italian flat leaf, flakes)	Slightly peppery; Italian parsley has a slightly stronger flavor	Garnish, herb mixtures, sauces, soups, stews
Rosemary (fresh and dried leaves)	Sweet, piney; reminiscent of pine needles	Casseroles, fish, lamb, salads, seafood, soups, vegetables
Sage (fresh and dried leaves, rubbed, ground)	Slightly musty, bitter; reminiscent of turkey stuffing	Fish, meats, poultry, salads, sausages, soups, stuffings
Savory (fresh, ground)	A cross between mint and thyme	Poultry, meats, salads, sauces, soups, stuffings, vegetables
Tarragon (fresh and dried leaves)	Astringent and aromatic; tastes like mild black licorice	Eggs, meats, pickling, poultry, salads, sauces, tomatoes
Thyme (fresh and dried leaves, ground)	Peppery, minty, light lemon flavor	Chowders, fish, meats, poultry, stews, stuffings, tomatoes

Spice Chart

SPICE AND FORM	FLAVOR	USE
Allspice (whole, ground; a spice, not a blend)	A cross between cloves and nutmeg; reminiscent of jerk chicken	Cakes, cookies, fruits, jerk seasoning, pickling, pies, poaching fish, spinach, stews
Cinnamon (stick, ground)	Sweet and woodsy; reminiscent of apple pie	Cakes, cappuccino, cookies, fruit desserts, hot chocolate, maple syrup, pies, pickling, puddings, winter hot drinks
Cloves (whole, ground)	Sweet, peppery; reminiscent of gingersnaps	Baked beans, desserts, fruits, gravies, ham, meats, pickling, pork, sausages, stews, syrups, tea, vegetables
Garlic (minced, powdered, dehydrated, flaked, fresh, paste, juice)	Slightly musty and reminiscent of garlic bread	Fish, meats, salads, sauces, sausages, soups, vegetables
Ginger (whole, cracked bits, ground, crystallized, fresh)	Spicy-hot and tangy; reminiscent of gingerbread	Baked goods, fish, fruits, meats, sauces, sausages, soups, tea, vegetables
Nutmeg (whole, ground; mace is the covering of the nutmeg seed and can be used the same way)	Sweet, spicy; reminiscent of eggnog	Apple or pear desserts, beverages, cakes, cookies, parsnips, puddings, sauces, sweet potatoes, winter squash
Paprika (ground; made from dried sweet red peppers)	Ranges from sweet to hot, slightly bitter; reminiscent of Hungarian goulash	Casseroles, eggs, fish, garnish, meats, salads, soups, vegetables
Pepper, black, white and green (whole, ground, cracked; green sold packed in brine or dried)	Slightly hot with a hint of sweetness; black pepper is the strongest, green is the mildest	Meats, savory foods
Pepper, red (cayenne; ground)	Very hot and peppery	Barbecue and other sauces, chili, corn bread, eggs, fish, gravies, guacamole, meats, vegetables
Saffron (strands, powdered)	Distinctive flavor, softly bitter; reminiscent of paella	Spanish dishes
Turmeric (ground)	Fragrant, woodsy; reminiscent of curry	Curry powder, eggs, food color, pickling, poultry, rice, seafood

Varieties of Natural Cheese

TEXTURE	FLAVOR	USE
VERY HARD (GRATING)		
Asiago	Sharp, slightly fruity	Cooking, seasoning
Parmesan	Sharp, salty	Cooking, pasta, salad, seasoning
Romano	Sharp, piquant, salty	Cooking, pasta, seasoning
HARD		
Cheddar	Rich, nutty, from mild to full-bodied bite	Cooking, dessert, with fruit
Cheshire	Tangy, salty	Cooking, with fruit
Edam, Gouda	Milky and nutty to sharp and salty	Appetizer, dessert
Gjetost	Sweet, fudgelike, caramely with a hint of condensed milk	Sandwich, snack
Gruyère	Mellow and buttery with a nutlike flavor	Cooking, dessert
Jarlsberg	Slightly sweet, nutty	Appetizer, sandwich, cooking
Nökkelost	Spiced with cloves, buttery	Appetizer, sandwich, cooking
Swiss	Mild, very fruity, mouth-tingling tang	Appetizer, cooking, dessert, sandwich
SEMISOFT		
Blue	Rich, robust, salty with a lingering tanginess	Appetizer, dessert, salad
Brick	From mild and sweet to savory with a spicy tang	Appetizer, sandwich
Colby	Mild and milky	Cooking, sandwich
Curds	Mild and milky, rubbery	Appetizer, snack
Feta	Very sharp, salty	Cooking, salad
Fontina	Delicate, nutty with a hint of honey	Appetizer, cooking
Gorgonzola	Earthy, rich, spicy	Dessert, salad
Havarti	Creamy, mild, smooth	Appetizer, cooking
Monterey Jack	Mild to mellow	Appetizer, cooking, sandwich
Mozzarella	Delicate, vaguely sweet and stringy	Appetizer, cooking, pizza
Muenster	Strong tasting and smelling, tangy, spicy	Appetizer, dessert, sandwich

Port du Salut	Nutty, almost meaty	Appetizer, dessert, sandwich
Provolone	Creamy, firm, slightly smoky	Cooking, sandwich
Reblochon	Mild with flavor of fresh-crushed walnuts	Appetizer, dessert
Roquefort	Rich, melt-in-your-mouth texture with a clean, sharp, lingering tang	Appetizer, dessert, salad
Stilton	Rich, spicy with a blended flavor of blue and Cheddar cheeses	Dessert, salad, snack
Taleggio	Full-bodied, creamy with a hint of asparagus	Appetizer, cooking

SOFT

Bel Paese	Rich, sweet, creamy, robust	Cooking, dessert
Boursin	Mild, rich, often seasoned with herbs or pepper	Appetizer
Brie	Mild, creamy, slight flavor of mushrooms	Appetizer, dessert
Bucheron	Mild, fresh, tangy	Cooking, dessert
Camembert	Creamy, slightly tangy, earthy	Appetizer, dessert, sandwich
Cottage, dry or creamed	Very bland, sometimes flavored	Cooking, salad
Cream	Rich, slightly tangy	Appetizer, dessert, salad
Farmer	Mild, fresh with a faintly sour tinge	Cooking
Liederkranz	Full-flavored, pungent, almost honeylike consistency	Appetizer, dessert
Limburger	Tangy, gamey and strong-smelling	Appetizer, snack
Mascarpone	Very soft, mild, sweet, almost like whipped cream	Dessert
Montrachet	Creamy, fresh, mildly tangy	Appetizer, cooking
Neufchâtel	Mild, rich with a hint of salt	Appetizer, dessert, salad, spread
Ricotta	Bland, slightly sweet	Cooking, dessert, pasta

Food Safety Basics

Beware the "Danger Zone"

The main difference between food-spoiling and food-poisoning bacteria is the temperatures at which they survive and grow. Bacteria that cause food to spoil can grow at refrigerator temperatures (below 40°F.). They usually make the food look or smell bad, which is an obvious clue to throw it out.

Most bacteria that cause food poisoning don't grow at refrigerator temperatures. The best temperature for these microorganisms to reproduce is around 100°F. But the actual temperature varies with the organism and may range from 40°F. to 140°F., or the "danger zone." These are pathogens, the type of bacteria that if eaten may lead to illness, disease or even death. The majority of them are invisible attackers; they can't be seen, smelled or tasted.
• Use paper towels when working with, or cleaning up after, raw foods, such as poultry and meats.
• Wash kitchen linen often because bacteria "hang out" in towels, sponges and cloths used over and over. Throw out dirty or mildewed dish sponges.

Three Basic Rules for Food Safety

The majority of food-poisoning bacteria can be controlled by cleaning, cooking and refrigeration. Follow these three rules to the letter when preparing food:
1. Keep everything in the kitchen *clean.*
2. Keep hot foods *hot.*
3. Keep cold foods *cold.*

Keep the Kitchen Clean

• Clean countertops, appliances, utensils and dishes with hot, soapy water or other cleaners, such as those labeled "antibacterial."
• Wash your hands thoroughly with soap and water for at least 20 seconds before handling food.
• Wash your hands and all utensils and surfaces with hot, soapy water after contact with raw poultry, meat, fish or seafood.
• If you have any kind of skin cut or infection on your hands, cover it with a bandage or wear protective plastic or rubber gloves.
• Hard plastic or glass cutting boards, because they're less porous than wooden boards, are recommended as the safest for raw poultry, meat, fish and seafood. Do not use wooden cutting boards for raw poultry, meat, fish or seafood. When your cutting board is battered with deep scratches and cuts, it's time to get a new one.
• Don't chop fresh vegetables, salad ingredients, fruit or any food that won't be fully cooked on a cutting board that was used for raw poultry, meat, fish or seafood without cleaning it as directed above. Wash any knives or utensils that were used in hot, soapy water.
• Don't transfer bacteria from raw meat to cooked meat. For example, don't carry raw hamburgers to the grill on a platter, then put the cooked burgers back on the same unwashed platter.

Keep Hot Food Hot

• Bacteria thrive at room temperature or in lukewarm food. So don't allow hot foods to stand at room temperature for more than 2 hours, including prep time. Keeping hot foods hot means keeping them at 140°F. or higher.
• Don't partially cook or heat perishable foods, then set them aside or refrigerate to finish cooking later. During cooking, the food may not reach a temperature high enough to destroy bacteria.
• Cook meat and poultry completely, following the "doneness" times and temperatures recommended.
• Reheat leftovers, stirring often, until "steaming" hot (165°F.). Do not taste leftover food that looks or smells strange to see if it's okay. When in doubt, throw it out!

Keep Cold Food Cold

• Bacteria thrive at room temperature, so don't allow cold foods to stand at room temperature for more than 2 hours, including prep time. Keeping cold foods cold means keeping them at 40°F. or lower.
• Foods chill faster if you allow space between them when stocking your refrigerator and freezer and if you divide large amounts into smaller ones and store foods in shallow containers.
• Buy a refrigerator thermometer to make sure your refrigerator is cooling at 35°F. to 40°F. Use a freezer thermometer to check that your freezer is maintaining 0°F. or colder. If your power goes out, keep the refrigerator doors closed to protect food up to 4 hours.
• Never thaw foods at room temperature—thaw only in the refrigerator or microwave. If you thaw foods in the microwave, finish cooking them immediately.

From the Kitchen of: _____

Recipe for: _____

_____

_____

_____

_____

_____

_____

_____

_____

_____

_____

_____

_____

_____

_____

_____

_____

_____

_____

_____

_____

_____

TM

From the Kitchen of: _____

Recipe for: _____

_____

_____

_____

_____

_____

_____

_____

_____

_____

_____

_____

_____

_____

_____

_____

_____

_____

_____

_____

TM

From the Kitchen of: _____

Recipe for: _____

_____

_____

_____

_____

_____

_____

_____

_____

_____

_____

_____

_____

_____

_____

_____

_____

_____

_____

_____

_____

_____

_____

TM

From the Kitchen of: _____

Recipe for: _____

_____
_____
_____
_____
_____
_____
_____
_____
_____
_____
_____
_____
_____
_____
_____
_____
_____
_____
_____
_____

™

From the Kitchen of: _____

Recipe for: _____

_____

_____

_____

_____

_____

_____

_____

_____

_____

_____

_____

_____

_____

_____

_____

_____

_____

_____

_____

_____

_____

TM

From the Kitchen of: _____

Recipe for: _____

_____

_____

_____

_____

_____

_____

_____

_____

_____

_____

_____

_____

_____

_____

_____

_____

_____

_____

_____

_____

_____

_____

TM

From the Kitchen of: _____

Recipe for: _____

_____

_____

_____

_____

_____

_____

_____

_____

_____

_____

_____

_____

_____

_____

_____

_____

_____

_____

_____

_____

_____

_____

TM

From the Kitchen of: _____

Recipe for: _____

_____
_____
_____
_____
_____
_____
_____
_____
_____
_____
_____
_____
_____
_____
_____
_____
_____
_____
_____
_____
_____

™

From the Kitchen of: _____

Recipe for: _____

_____

_____

_____

_____

_____

_____

_____

_____

_____

_____

_____

_____

_____

_____

_____

_____

_____

_____

_____

_____

TM

From the Kitchen of: _____

Recipe for: _____

_____

_____

_____

_____

_____

_____

_____

_____

_____

_____

_____

_____

_____

_____

_____

_____

_____

_____

_____

_____

_____

_____

TM

From the Kitchen of: _____

Recipe for: _____

_____

_____

_____

_____

_____

_____

_____

_____

_____

_____

_____

_____

_____

_____

_____

_____

_____

_____

_____

_____

_____

TM

From the Kitchen of: _____

Recipe for: _____

_____

_____

_____

_____

_____

_____

_____

_____

_____

_____

_____

_____

_____

_____

_____

_____

_____

_____

_____

_____

_____

TM

From the Kitchen of: _____

Recipe for: _____

_____

_____

_____

_____

_____

_____

_____

_____

_____

_____

_____

_____

_____

_____

_____

_____

_____

_____

_____

_____

_____

TM

From the Kitchen of: _____

Recipe for: _____

_____

_____

_____

_____

_____

_____

_____

_____

_____

_____

_____

_____

_____

_____

_____

_____

_____

_____

_____

_____

_____

TM

From the Kitchen of: _____

Recipe for: _____

_____

_____

_____

_____

_____

_____

_____

_____

_____

_____

_____

_____

_____

_____

_____

_____

_____

_____

_____

_____

_____

TM

From the Kitchen of: _____

Recipe for: _____

_____
_____
_____
_____
_____
_____
_____
_____
_____
_____
_____
_____
_____
_____
_____
_____
_____
_____
_____
_____

TM

From the Kitchen of: _____

Recipe for: _____

_____

_____

_____

_____

_____

_____

_____

_____

_____

_____

_____

_____

_____

_____

_____

_____

_____

_____

_____

_____

_____

™

From the Kitchen of: _____

Recipe for: _____

_____

_____

_____

_____

_____

_____

_____

_____

_____

_____

_____

_____

_____

_____

_____

_____

_____

_____

_____

™

From the Kitchen of: _____

Recipe for: _____

_____

_____

_____

_____

_____

_____

_____

_____

_____

_____

_____

_____

_____

_____

_____

_____

_____

_____

_____

From the Kitchen of: _____

Recipe for: _____

_____
_____
_____
_____
_____
_____
_____
_____
_____
_____
_____
_____
_____
_____
_____
_____
_____
_____
_____
_____
_____
_____
_____

™

From the Kitchen of: _____

Recipe for: _____

_____

_____

_____

_____

_____

_____

_____

_____

_____

_____

_____

_____

_____

_____

_____

_____

_____

_____

_____

_____

TM

From the Kitchen of: _____

Recipe for: _____

_____

_____

_____

_____

_____

_____

_____

_____

_____

_____

_____

_____

_____

_____

_____

_____

_____

_____

_____

_____

_____

TM

From the Kitchen of: _____

Recipe for: _____

_____

_____

_____

_____

_____

_____

_____

_____

_____

_____

_____

_____

_____

_____

_____

_____

_____

_____

From the Kitchen of: _____

Recipe for: _____

_____
_____
_____
_____
_____
_____
_____
_____
_____
_____
_____
_____
_____
_____
_____
_____
_____
_____
_____
_____
_____

TM

From the Kitchen of: _____

Recipe for: _____

_____

_____

_____

_____

_____

_____

_____

_____

_____

_____

_____

_____

_____

_____

_____

_____

_____

_____

_____

_____

™

From the Kitchen of: _____

Recipe for: _____

_____

_____

_____

_____

_____

_____

_____

_____

_____

_____

_____

_____

_____

_____

_____

_____

_____

_____

TM

From the Kitchen of: _____

Recipe for: _____

_____

_____

_____

_____

_____

_____

_____

_____

_____

_____

_____

_____

_____

_____

_____

_____

_____

_____

_____

_____

TM

From the Kitchen of: _____

Recipe for: _____

_____

_____

_____

_____

_____

_____

_____

_____

_____

_____

_____

_____

_____

_____

_____

_____

_____

_____

_____

_____

TM

From the Kitchen of: _____

Recipe for: _____

_____

_____

_____

_____

_____

_____

_____

_____

_____

_____

_____

_____

_____

_____

_____

_____

_____

_____

_____

_____

_____

_____

_____

TM

From the Kitchen of: _____

Recipe for: _____

_____

_____

_____

_____

_____

_____

_____

_____

_____

_____

_____

_____

_____

_____

_____

_____

_____

_____

_____

_____

_____

TM

From the Kitchen of: _____

Recipe for: _____

_____

_____

_____

_____

_____

_____

_____

_____

_____

_____

_____

_____

_____

_____

_____

_____

_____

_____

_____

_____

_____

_____

™

From the Kitchen of: _____

Recipe for: _____

_____

_____

_____

_____

_____

_____

_____

_____

_____

_____

_____

_____

_____

_____

_____

_____

_____

_____

_____

_____

_____

™

From the Kitchen of: _____

Recipe for: _____

_____
_____
_____
_____
_____
_____
_____
_____
_____
_____
_____
_____
_____
_____
_____
_____
_____
_____
_____
_____
_____
_____

TM

From the Kitchen of: _____

Recipe for: _____

_____

_____

_____

_____

_____

_____

_____

_____

_____

_____

_____

_____

_____

_____

_____

_____

_____

_____

_____

_____

_____

TM

From the Kitchen of: _____

Recipe for: _____

_____

_____

_____

_____

_____

_____

_____

_____

_____

_____

_____

_____

_____

_____

_____

_____

_____

_____

_____

_____

TM

From the Kitchen of: _____

Recipe for: _____

_____

_____

_____

_____

_____

_____

_____

_____

_____

_____

_____

_____

_____

_____

_____

_____

_____

_____

_____

_____

_____

_____

™

From the Kitchen of: _____

Recipe for: _____

_____

_____

_____

_____

_____

_____

_____

_____

_____

_____

_____

_____

_____

_____

_____

_____

_____

_____

_____

_____

™

From the Kitchen of: _____

Recipe for: _____

_____

_____

_____

_____

_____

_____

_____

_____

_____

_____

_____

_____

_____

_____

_____

_____

_____

_____

_____

TM

From the Kitchen of: _____

Recipe for: _____

_____

_____

_____

_____

_____

_____

_____

_____

_____

_____

_____

_____

_____

_____

_____

_____

_____

_____

_____

_____

TM

From the Kitchen of: _____

Recipe for: _____

_____

_____

_____

_____

_____

_____

_____

_____

_____

_____

_____

_____

_____

_____

_____

_____

_____

_____

_____

_____

TM

From the Kitchen of: _____

Recipe for: _____

_____

_____

_____

_____

_____

_____

_____

_____

_____

_____

_____

_____

_____

_____

_____

_____

_____

_____

_____

TM

From the Kitchen of: _____

Recipe for: _____

_____
_____
_____
_____
_____
_____
_____
_____
_____
_____
_____
_____
_____
_____
_____
_____
_____
_____
_____
_____
_____

™

From the Kitchen of: _____

Recipe for: _____

_____

_____

_____

_____

_____

_____

_____

_____

_____

_____

_____

_____

_____

_____

_____

_____

_____

_____

_____

_____

_____

TM

From the Kitchen of: _____

Recipe for: _____

_____
_____
_____
_____
_____
_____
_____
_____
_____
_____
_____
_____
_____
_____
_____
_____
_____
_____
_____
_____
_____

™

From the Kitchen of: _____

Recipe for: _____

_____
_____
_____
_____
_____
_____
_____
_____
_____
_____
_____
_____
_____
_____
_____
_____
_____
_____
_____
_____
_____
_____

TM

From the Kitchen of: _____

Recipe for: _____

_____

_____

_____

_____

_____

_____

_____

_____

_____

_____

_____

_____

_____

_____

_____

_____

_____

_____

_____

_____

TM

From the Kitchen of: _____

Recipe for: _____

_____

_____

_____

_____

_____

_____

_____

_____

_____

_____

_____

_____

_____

_____

_____

_____

_____

_____

_____

_____

TM

From the Kitchen of: _____

Recipe for: _____

_____

_____

_____

_____

_____

_____

_____

_____

_____

_____

_____

_____

_____

_____

_____

_____

_____

_____

_____

_____

TM

From the Kitchen of: _____

Recipe for: _____

_____

_____

_____

_____

_____

_____

_____

_____

_____

_____

_____

_____

_____

_____

_____

_____

_____

_____

_____

_____

_____

TM

From the Kitchen of: _____

Recipe for: _____

_____

_____

_____

_____

_____

_____

_____

_____

_____

_____

_____

_____

_____

_____

_____

_____

_____

_____

_____

_____

_____

_____

_____

TM

Cranberry-Glazed Appetizer Meatballs

MEATBALLS
- 1¹/₂ lb. lean ground beef
- ¹/₂ cup finely chopped onion
- ¹/₂ cup Progresso® Plain Bread Crumbs
- ¹/₂ teaspoon salt
- ¹/₈ teaspoon pepper
- 2 eggs, slightly beaten

SAUCE
- 1 (12-oz.) bottle (1¹/₂ cups) chili sauce
- 1 (8-oz.) can (about 1 cup) jellied cranberry sauce

1. Heat oven to 375°F. In large bowl, combine all meatball ingredients; mix well. Shape into 60 (1-inch) balls; place in ungreased 15×10×1-inch baking pan.

2. Bake at 375°F. for 25 to 30 minutes or until meatballs are thoroughly cooked and no longer pink in center.

3. Meanwhile, in large saucepan, combine sauce ingredients; blend well. Bring to a boil over medium heat. Reduce heat to low; simmer 5 minutes, stirring occasionally.

60 meatballs; 30 servings

Mini Swiss Quiches

- 1 (15-oz.) pkg. Pillsbury® Refrigerated Pie Crusts, softened as directed on package
- 6 oz. (1¹/₂ cups) shredded Swiss Cheese
- 2 tablespoons sliced green onions
- 1 tablespoon chopped pimientos
- 2 eggs
- ¹/₂ cup milk
- ¹/₄ teaspoon salt
- Dash nutmeg

1. Heat oven to 375°F. Spray 24 miniature muffin cups with nonstick cooking spray. Remove pie crusts from pouches. Unfold 1 pie crust; press out fold lines. With floured 2 1/2-inch round cutter, cut 12 rounds. Press each round in bottom and up sides of sprayed muffin cup. Repeat with second crust.

2. Place 1 tablespoon cheese in each cup. Top each with a few onion slices and pimiento pieces.

3. In 2-cup measuring cup, combine eggs, milk, salt and nutmeg; beat well with fork. Pour mixture into crust-lined cups, filling each to within 1/4 inch of top.

4. Bake at 375°F. for 25 to 30 minutes or until golden brown. Cool slightly; lift quiches from cups with tip of knife. Serve warm.

24 appetizers

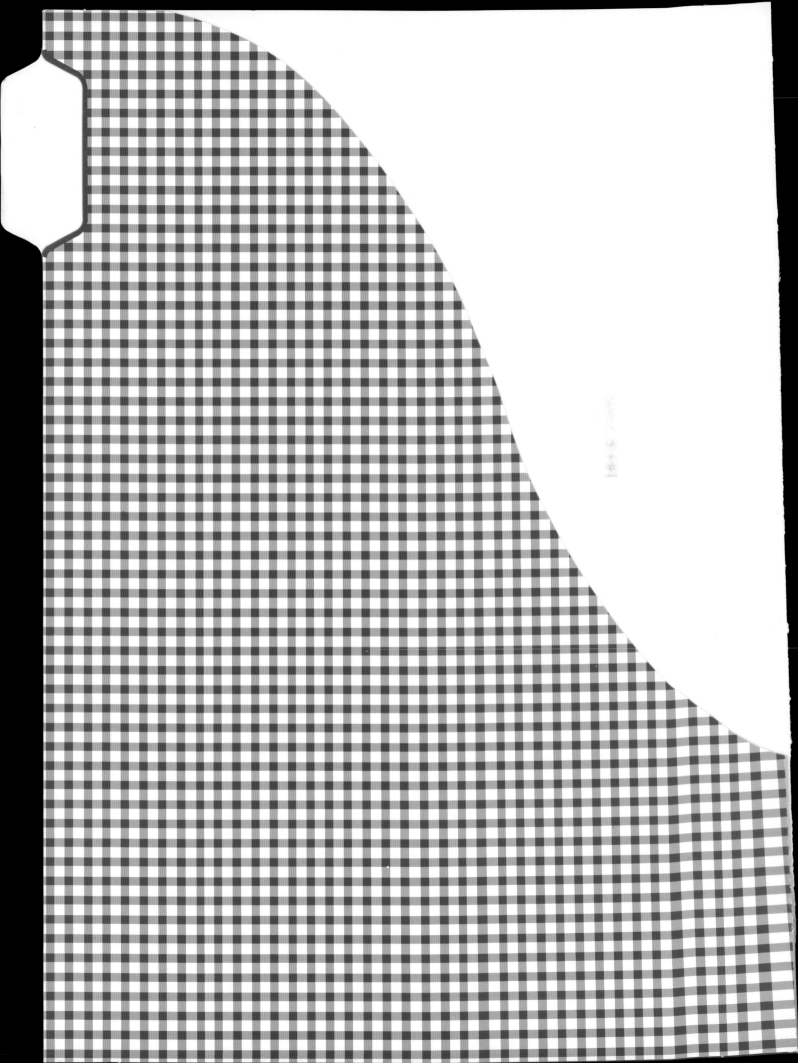

Bread Bowl Chili

Bread Tips
Choose a hearty bread that feels heavy for its size. Pumpernickel raisin, corn rye or sourdough bread are good choices. If the texture of the bread is too soft, the chili will be absorbed too quickly.

Serving Idea
Serve this chili as a winter warmer lunch. Make the chili the night before. Reheat just before you are ready to serve. Along with a dollop of sour cream, garnish the chili with shredded cheddar cheese and chopped cilantro.

COOKING TIME
40 minutes

GOOD IDEA For extra spice, add $1/4$ teaspoon of cayenne pepper to the chili when simmering.

Variations

Simply Chili
Of course, this chili can also be served without the bread bowl. Serve the chili over rice or noodles to make a complete meal.

A Great Duo
Fill a bread bowl with your favorite chunky beef stew. The bread will absorb some of the flavor of the stew, making for a great accompaniment.

You Will Need

FOR THE BREAD BOWL
- 1 large round bread loaf

FOR THE CHILI
- 1 medium jalapeño pepper, diced
- 12 ounces lean ground beef
- 2 teaspoons olive oil
- 2 medium yellow onions, chopped (about 2 cups)
- 1 medium green bell pepper, chopped (about 1 cup)
- 1 tablespoon chili powder
- 1 can (14½ ounces) whole tomatoes
- ¼ cup no-salt-added tomato paste
- 1 can (8½ ounces) red kidney beans, drained and rinsed
- 1 can (7 ounces) whole kernel corn, drained

SERVES 4

Kitchen Tips

Once you serve the chili, slice the bread bowl into wedges and serve. The flavor of the chili gives the bread an added zest.

Step by Step

MAKING THE BREAD BOWL

1. Using a serrated knife, slice off about an inch from the top of the bread.

2. Carve out a "bowl" from within the bread, leaving about 1 inch inside. ▼

MAKING THE CHILI

1. To chop jalapeño pepper, use a knife and fork to hold in place. Chop pepper into fine pieces. Avoid touching seeds with your hands. ▼

2. In a large nonstick skillet, cook beef over medium heat, stirring, until browned, about 5 minutes. Drain beef.

3. In same skillet, heat oil over medium heat. Add onions; cook, stirring, for 5 minutes. Add bell pepper, jalapeño pepper and chili powder; cook, stirring, for 5 minutes.

4. Add beef, tomatoes with liquid and tomato paste; bring to a boil. Reduce heat to low; simmer for 25 minutes. Add beans and corn; cook 5 minutes longer.

5. Ladle chili into bread bowl and serve immediately. ▼

Attention to Detail

Another popular dish to serve in a bread bowl is Creamy Spinach Dip. The inside of the bread is cubed and served alongside the dip.

CREAMY SPINACH DIP
- 1 cup frozen chopped spinach, thawed and drained
- 1 cup sour cream
- ½ cup cottage cheese
- 1 tablespoon dried onion flakes
- 1 teaspoon lemon juice
- salt and pepper to taste

Combine all ingredients in a large bowl. Chill for 2 hours. Return to room temperature before serving.

Rib Roast Dinner

GOOD IDEA Use leftover roast beef to make hearty sandwiches for the next day's lunch.

Variations

An Appetizer to Please
Stuff small red potatoes instead of the russets and serve them as a snack or appetizer. They are delicious!

A Tasty Idea
Substitute large sweet potatoes for the russets. Try Monterey Jack cheese on top instead of Colby.

You Will Need

FOR THE POTATOES

- 6 large russet potatoes, scrubbed
- 1 tablespoon butter or margarine
- ½ cup diced red bell pepper
- ½ cup diced green bell pepper
- ⅔ cup chopped yellow onion
- 4 slices baked ham (about 4 ounces), diced
- 1½ cups shredded Colby cheese, divided
- 2 tablespoons milk
- 2 tablespoons sour cream

FOR THE ROAST

- 1 tablespoon coarsely cracked black pepper
- 1 2¼-pound boneless rib roast or tenderloin
- ¼ cup fresh flat-leaf parsley
- 1 tablespoon fresh chives
- 1 tablespoon fresh tarragon leaves
- 1 teaspoon dried thyme

SERVES 6

Kitchen Tips

Do not tie the beef too tightly with twine or the flavorful meat juices might escape.

Step by Step

MAKING THE POTATOES

1. Preheat oven to 400°F. Pierce potatoes several times with a fork. Bake until tender, about 1 hour. Meanwhile, melt butter in a large nonstick skillet set over medium heat. Add peppers and onion; sauté until tender, about 5 minutes. Add ham; sauté for 5 minutes.

2. Reduce temperature to 350°F. Cool potatoes slightly. Slice tops off potatoes and scoop out pulp; reserve skins. In a bowl, mash pulp. Stir in 1 cup Colby, milk, sour cream and vegetable mixture. Spoon mixture into potato shells.

3. Sprinkle potatoes with remaining Colby. Place on baking sheet. Bake until heated through, about 20 minutes. Serve with roast.

MAKING THE ROAST

1. Increase oven temperature to 425°F. Rub the pepper evenly over beef, pressing gently so pepper adheres.

2. Place the herbs in a large measuring cup and chop using kitchen shears. ▼

3. On a sheet of waxed paper, combi fresh and dried herbs. Roll beef in her mixture to completely coat. ▼

4. Loosely tie the beef at 2-inch intervals with kitchen twine. Place bee on roasting rack. ▼

5. Roast until an instant-read meat thermometer registers 155°F. for medium, about 30 minutes. Let stand for 5 minutes; carve into thin slices.

Attention to Detail

Use a meat thermometer to check the doneness of the beef.

For rare	130°F
For medium	155°F
For well-done	170°F

Fancy Roast Chicken Dinner

Time Saver
Cook the chicken without stuffing and cut down on cooking time. Make a quick stove-cooked stuffing to serve on the side.

Make Ahead
Use your favorite stuffing recipe and make it ahead of time. Place cooled stuffing in a bowl. Cover the bowl with plastic wrap and refrigerate for up to 2 days.

Best Steaming
When steaming vegetables, make sure you have a tightly-sealed lid to ensure even cooking.

**ROASTING TIME
2 hours**

GOOD IDEA Serve a refreshing sorbet or sherbet for an easy dessert.

Variations

Company Fare
For a change of pace, serve 3 roasted Cornish hens that have been filled with stuffing.

Garlic Spread
Roast some extra garlic and refrigerate in an airtight container to use as a spread for toasted bread slices.

You Will Need

FOR THE ROAST CHICKEN

- 3 cups seasoned bread stuffing
- 1 roasting chicken (about 7 pounds)
- 1 teaspoon salt
- 1 teaspoon black pepper

FOR THE ROAST GARLIC

- 4 tablespoons melted butter
- ¼ cup olive oil
- 3 heads of garlic

FOR THE VEGETABLE BUNDLES

- 1 large carrot
- 1 pound green beans, steamed
- 1 bunch green onions, stalks only, blanched

SERVES 6

Kitchen Tips

- To steam green beans, bring a little water to a boil in a large saucepan. Place green beans in a steamer basket and place basket in pan. Steam, covered, just until tender, about 5 minutes.
- To blanch green onion stalks, plunge stalks into boiling water until they become limp, about 5 seconds. Plunge into ice water and drain.

Step by Step

ROASTING THE CHICKEN

1. Preheat oven to 350°F. Prepare stuffing according to package directions. Sprinkle chicken with salt and pepper. Spoon stuffing into cavity. Tie legs together.

2. Place chicken on rack in a roasting pan. Roast until meat thermometer inserted in thickest part of thigh registers 180°F., about 2 hours.

ROASTING THE GARLIC

1. To roast the garlic, in a small bowl, combine butter and olive oil. Cut garlic heads in half; do not peel.

2. Brush butter mixture over cut garlic heads. Place garlic on a small baking sheet. Roast alongside chicken. ▼

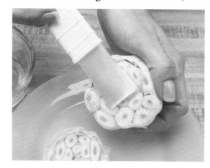

MAKING THE VEGETABLE BUNDLES

1. Fill a medium bowl with ice water. Using a vegetable peeler, or a sharp paring knife, peel carrot into very thin strips. In a small saucepan, bring water to boil.

2. Drop carrot strips into boiling water until they become limp, about 10 seconds. Remove strips and plunge into ice water; set aside. ▼

3. Gather some green beans; wrap a carrot strip around each bunch and tie with blanched green onion stalk. ▼

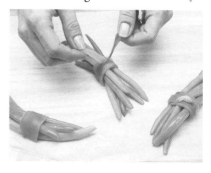

SERVING THE CHICKEN

1. Transfer chicken to a serving platter; let stand for 15 minutes before carving. Transfer stuffing to a serving bowl.

2. Arrange green bean bundles around chicken. Place roasted garlic heads on a decorative plate.

Vegetable Party Bouquet

Make Ahead
Chop and carve the vegetables up to 1 day in advance. Store in a bowl of ice water in the refrigerator.

Go-Withs
Offer these tasty vegetables with a cheesy herb dip and some crisp sesame crackers. For a main meal, serve bouquet with your favorite soup and some bread.

Easy Substitute
If you have trouble finding some of these vegetables, use olives, yellow squash and green peppers.

PREPARATION TIME
45 minutes

GOOD IDEA For a decorative touch, blanch the vegetables and serve them alongside a tender beef roast or turkey.

Variations

A Simple Circle
Arrange sliced rounds of cucumbers, various peppers and endive spears in overlapping circles. Fill in the center with broccoli florets and diced peppers.

The Square Root
A brightly-colored square platter, filled with colorful cut-up vegetables arranged in a tic-tac-toe grid, makes a stunning and tasty presentation.

You Will Need

FOR THE BASE

- 1 large head of cabbage

FOR THE BOUQUET

- 1 bunch radishes
- 1 yellow bell pepper
- 1 orange bell pepper
- 5 medium carrots
- 2 bunches green onions
- 2 cups broccoli florets
- 2 cups cauliflower florets
- 1 cucumber, sliced into rounds
- 1 pint cherry tomatoes
- 5 stalks celery with tops
- 1 small head endive
- 1 bunch chicory
- 1 bunch asparagus spears, blanched
- 1 box thin Italian breadsticks

SPECIAL AIDS

bamboo skewers
1 large basket, 2 inches deep

SERVES 14

Kitchen Tips

- To keep the breadsticks from getting soggy, add them to the arrangement just before serving.
- Use a paring knife to carve all vegetables.

Step by Step

PREPARING THE VEGETABLES

1. Cut off ends of each radish. Slice halfway down on four sides to form petals. Place in bowl of ice water. ▼

2. Core bell peppers; cut into vertical leaf-shaped slices. Make tulips from carrots (see Attention to Detail).

3. Cut off the bottom of the green onion stalks (about 3 inches); reserve upper portions. Make close vertical slits, from cut end down to an inch from base. Place in ice water to frill.

ASSEMBLING THE BOUQUET

1. Trim skewers to various lengths. Place leftover green onion stalks over some skewers like a sheath. ▼

2. Insert tops of sheathed skewers into bottoms of all florets, pepper and cucumber slices, radish and carrot flowers, tomatoes, prepared green onions, celery stalks and endive and chicory leaves. Insert unsheathed skewers into asparagus spears and breadsticks.

3. Cut cabbage in half; place in bottom of basket. To form a pleasing rounded bouquet, insert ends of skewers into cabbage, balancing shapes and colors of vegetables. Place vegetables on shorter skewers along outer rim of basket. ▼

Attention to Detail

- To make carrot tulips, slice toward pointed end of carrot with tip of paring knife to form a petal; do not cut through. Form two more petals around carrot.

- Angle knife tip to separate flower from rest of carrot. Continue cutting out more tulips from carrot.

Baja Chicken Salad with Taco Vinaigrette

- 1 (1.25-oz.) pkg. Old El Paso® Taco Seasoning Mix
- 1 tablespoon brown sugar
- 1/2 cup cider vinegar
- 1/2 cup oil
- 4 boneless skinless chicken breast halves, cut into 1-inch pieces
- 1 to 2 tablespoons oil
- 1 (10-oz.) pkg. mixed salad greens or baby greens
- 1 cup grape tomatoes, halved
- 1/2 cup sliced red onion
- 2 2/3 oz. (2/3 cup) shredded Cheddar-Monterey Jack cheese blend
- 1/3 cup sour cream
- 1 avocado, pitted, peeled and sliced
- 3 tablespoons sliced ripe olives
  Blue tortilla chips

1. In medium bowl, combine taco seasoning mix, brown sugar, vinegar and 1/2 cup oil; mix well. Place chicken in shallow medium bowl. Pour 1/2 cup seasoning mixture over chicken. Reserve remaining mixture for dressing.
2. Heat 1 to 2 tablespoons oil in medium nonstick skillet over medium-high heat until hot. With slotted spoon, remove chicken from seasoning mixture; discard remaining seasoning mixture. Add chicken to skillet; cook and stir 5 minutes or until no longer pink in center.
3. In large bowl, combine mixed greens, tomatoes and onion. Add reserved seasoning mixture; toss to coat. Arrange salad mixture on serving platter. Top with chicken, cheese, sour cream, avocado and olives. Arrange tortilla chips around salad.

6 servings

Easy Corn Chowder

- 1 (11-oz.) can Green Giant® Niblets® Whole Kernel Corn, undrained
- 1/2 cup chopped onion
- 1/2 cup cubed peeled potatoes
- 1/3 cup water
- 2 teaspoons chicken-flavor instant bouillon
- 1 3/4 cups milk
- 1 tablespoon butter or margarine
- 2 tablespoons all-purpose flour

1. In large saucepan, combine corn, onion, potatoes, water and bouillon. Bring to a boil. Reduce heat to low; cover and simmer 10 minutes or until potatoes are tender, stirring occasionally.
2. Stir in 1 1/2 cups of the milk and the butter. In small bowl, combine remaining 1/4 cup milk and the flour; beat with wire whisk until smooth. Add flour mixture to chowder; cook and stir until bubbly and thickened.

3 (1-cup) servings

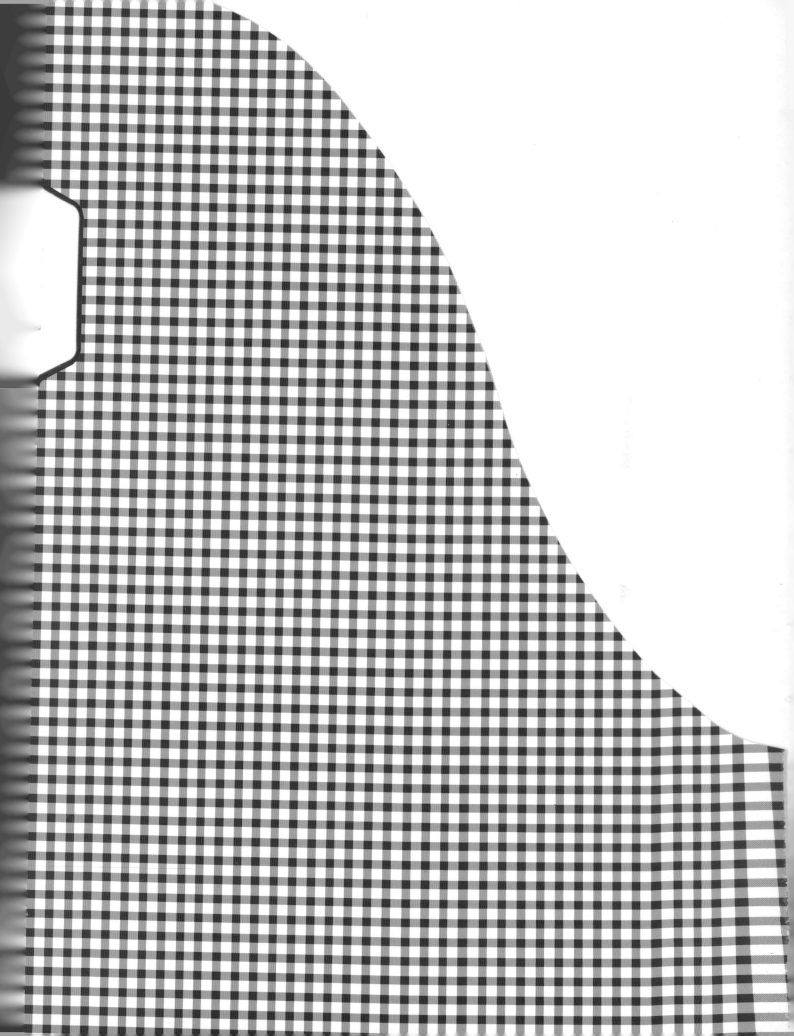

White Chicken Chili

1 tablespoon oil
1 cup chopped onions
2 garlic cloves, minced
1 lb. boneless skinless chicken breasts, cut into bite-sized pieces
3 (14-oz.) cans chicken broth
2 (15-oz.) cans cannellini beans, drained
2 (4.5-oz.) cans Old El Paso® Chopped Green Chiles, drained
1 teaspoon dried oregano leaves
1/2 teaspoon cumin
Dash ground red pepper (cayenne), if desired
6 oz. (1 1/2 cups) shredded Monterey Jack cheese
Chopped fresh cilantro, if desired

1. Heat oil in large saucepan or Dutch oven over medium-high heat until hot. Add onions, garlic and chicken; cook and stir until chicken is no longer pink.
2. Stir in all remaining ingredients except cheese and cilantro. Bring to a boil. Reduce heat to low; simmer 10 to 15 minutes to blend flavors, stirring occasionally.
3. To serve, spoon chili into soup bowls. Top each serving with cheese and cilantro.

9 (1-cup) servings

Zesty Italian Crescent Casserole

1 lb. lean ground beef
1/4 cup chopped onion
1 cup tomato pasta sauce
6 oz. (1 1/2 cups) shredded mozzarella or Monterey Jack cheese
1/2 cup sour cream
1 (8-oz.) can Pillsbury® Refrigerated Crescent Dinner Rolls
1/3 cup grated Parmesan cheese
2 tablespoons butter or margarine, melted

1. Heat oven to 375°F. In large skillet, cook ground beef and onion over medium heat for 8 to 10 minutes or until beef is thoroughly cooked, stirring frequently. Drain. Stir in pasta sauce; cook until thoroughly heated.
2. Meanwhile, in medium bowl, combine mozzarella cheese and sour cream; mix well.
3. Pour hot beef mixture into ungreased 9 1/2- or 10-inch glass deep-dish pie pan or 11×7-inch (2-quart) glass baking dish. Spoon cheese mixture over beef mixture.
4. Unroll dough over cheese mixture. (If using pie pan, separate dough into 8 triangles; arrange points toward center over cheese mixture, crimping outside edges if necessary.) In small bowl, mix Parmesan cheese and butter. Spread evenly over dough.
5. Bake at 375°F. for 18 to 25 minutes or until deep golden brown.

6 servings

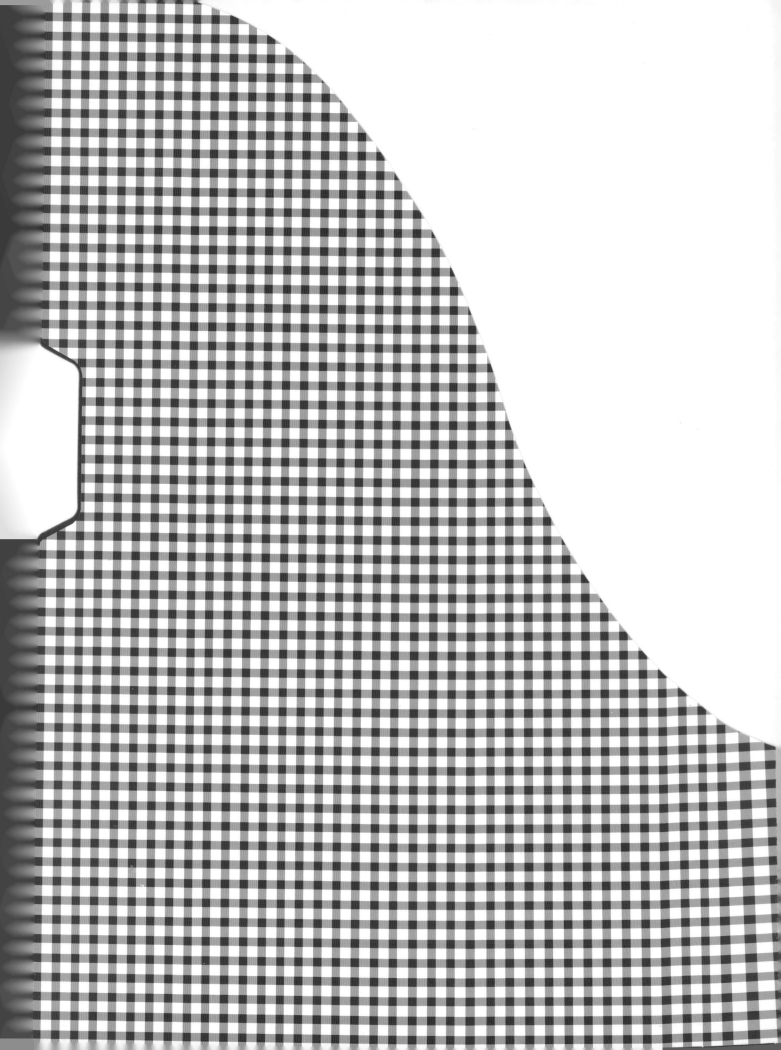

Mandarin Orange-Corn Slaw

SALAD

3 cups purchased three-color coleslaw blend

3 tablespoons chopped green onions, reserving 1 green top for garnish

1 (11-oz.) can Green Giant® Mexicorn® Whole Kernel Corn, Red and Green Peppers, drained

1 (11-oz.) can mandarin orange segments, drained, reserving 6 to 8 segments for garnish

DRESSING

1/2 cup light mayonnaise

2 tablespoons sugar

1 tablespoon red wine vinegar

1 tablespoon lime juice

1. In large bowl, combine all salad ingredients except reserved onion top and reserved orange segments; mix well. In small bowl, combine all dressing ingredients; blend well.

2. Add dressing to salad; toss to coat. Serve immediately, or cover and refrigerate until serving time.

3. To make flower garnish, cut lengthwise slits, 2/3 of the way down, in reserved green onion top; curve strips to resemble leaves. Arrange reserved mandarin orange segments on top of leaves to resemble flower petals.

8 (1/2-cup) servings

Havarti Ham and Potatoes

1 (10 1/4-oz.) can condensed cream of celery soup

1/2 cup sour cream with chives and onions (from 8-oz. container)

4 oz. (1 cup) shredded Havarti cheese

1 (1 lb. 4-oz.) pkg. refrigerated unpeeled potato wedges

1 1/2 cups cubed cooked ham

1 cup Green Giant Select® LeSueur® Frozen Baby Sweet Peas (from 1-lb. pkg.)

1 cup french fried onions

1. Heat oven to 350°F. Spray shallow 2-quart casserole with nonstick cooking spray. In large bowl, combine soup, sour cream and cheese; mix well. Add potatoes, ham and peas; stir gently to mix. Spoon into sprayed casserole. Cover.

2. Bake covered at 350°F. for 30 minutes.

3. Uncover casserole; sprinkle french fried onions over top. Bake uncovered an additional 25 to 30 minutes or until bubbly and thoroughly heated.

4 (1 3/4-cup) servings

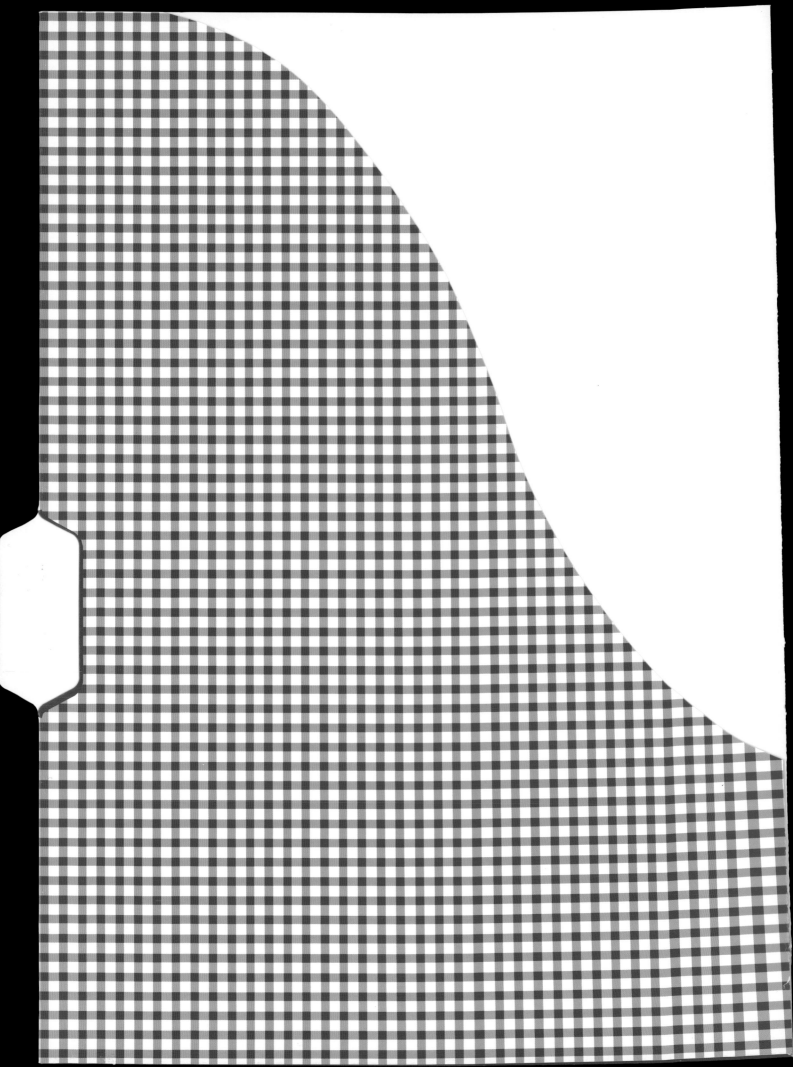

Fruit Salad Basket

Make Ahead
Make the fruit salad portion up to 1 day ahead. Cover with plastic wrap and refrigerate.

Easy Substitute
Kiwifruit, peeled and cut into quarters, makes a delicious substitute for the berries in this recipe.

Simple Elegance
Offer this fruit salad as a tasty dessert. Serve it, without the melon basket, in small crystal bowls. Top with a small mound of lemon sorbet and garnish with a sprig of mint.

**PREPARATION TIME
45 minutes**

GOOD IDEA Use the fruit salad to create colorful ice cubes. Serve them with fruit punch or lemonade for a cool treat.

Variations

For a Children's Party
To make a whale-shaped watermelon bowl, first sketch the body design on the melon; use a sharp knife to cut it out. Use celery stalks for the water spout.

Baby Shower Idea
For a baby shower, make this clever baby carriage basket. Shape excess rind into a handle and attach grapefruit halves for wheels.

You Will Need

FOR THE FRUIT SALAD

- 1 **large watermelon (about 15 pounds)**
- 2 **cantaloupe melons**
- 2 **honeydew melons**
- ½ **cup sugar**
- ½ **cup fresh lime juice**
- ¼ **cup fresh lemon juice**
- 2 **tablespoons orange-flavored liqueur (optional)**
- 2 **teaspoons grated lime peel**
- 3 **cups sliced fresh strawberries, washed, hulled and halved**
- 2 **cups black or red seedless grapes, washed and halved**

SPECIAL AIDS

water-soluble marker
melon baller
vegetable peeler

SERVES 18

Kitchen Tips

It's important to purchase watermelons that are fully ripe, since they don't continue to ripen once they've been picked. A ripe melon feels heavy for its size and has a sweet, fresh fragrance.

Step by Step

CARVING THE BASKET

1. Lay a dampened dish towel on a counter or table and place melon on top to prevent it from rolling.

2. With a water-soluble marker, draw outline of basket onto melon, making sure the handle is at least 1¼ inches wide. ▼

3. Using a large sharp knife, carefully cut melon along marker line. ▼

4. Remove excess rind and set aside. With a melon baller, scoop out all the watermelon flesh and place in a large glass or ceramic bowl; set aside.

5. With a vegetable peeler, even out scalloped edges of watermelon. Cover watermelon basket with clear plastic wrap and set aside. ▼

MAKING THE FRUIT SALAD

1. With a melon baller, scoop out flesh from cantaloupes and honeydews.

2. In a large bowl, combine sugar, lime juice, lemon juice, orange liqueur and lime peel. Stir well.

3. Add all melon balls, strawberries and grapes; toss to combine. Allow fruit to chill in refrigerator for 30 minutes.

4. Just before serving, transfer fruit salad to watermelon basket.

Attention to Detail

Follow any one of these decorative patterns to carve the edge of your watermelon basket.

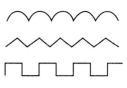

The Ultimate Cheesecake

Make Ahead
Cheesecakes are perfect desserts to make ahead. Wrap an undecorated cake in foil and store in the refrigerator for up to 4 days.

Seasonal Idea
If fresh blueberries are in season, add a decorative berry border around the bottom edge of the cheesecake as an edible garnish.

Lighten Up
Cut the amount of fat and calories in this recipe by using low-fat cream cheese.

BAKING TIME
1 hour 35 minutes
plus standing

GOOD IDEA To spice up the crust, replace the graham cracker crumbs with an equal amount of crushed gingersnaps.

Variations

Fruit Rings
Arrange multicolored fruits in concentric rings around the cake. Start with peach slices, followed by overlapping pineapple, kiwifruit and grapes.

A Fruit Blossom
Create the look of a chrysanthemum blossom with overlapping mandarin orange sections and a mound of fresh raspberries.

You Will Need

FOR THE CRUST

- 1½ cups graham cracker crumbs
- 2 tablespoons sugar
- ¼ cup (½ stick) butter or margarine, melted

FOR THE FILLING

- 5 packages (8 ounces each) cream cheese, softened
- 1⅓ cups sugar
- 3 tablespoons all-purpose flour
- 3 large eggs
- ½ cup sour cream
- 2 teaspoons finely grated lemon peel
- 1½ teaspoons vanilla extract

FOR THE TOPPING

- 1 egg white
- 1 tablespoon sugar
- ½ cup sour cream
- ½ cup raspberry preserves
- ½ cup apricot preserves
- 1 cup assorted fresh fruit, chopped

SERVES 16

Kitchen Tips

Use a smooth measuring cup to help press crumbs evenly against sides and bottom of springform pan.

Step by Step

PREPARING THE CRUST

1. In a medium bowl, combine graham cracker crumbs and sugar. Add melted butter; stir to combine.

2. Press crumb mixture into a 9-inch springform pan. Chill 30 minutes. ▼

MAKING THE FILLING

1. Preheat oven to 325°F. In a large bowl, using an electric mixer set on medium speed, beat cream cheese for 2 minutes; add sugar.

2. Gradually add flour; mix until combined. On low speed, beat in eggs, one at a time, until just blended.

3. Add sour cream, lemon peel and vanilla; beat until just blended. Pour into crust. Bake for 1 hour 15 minutes. Remove cake from oven; cool for 15 minutes.

4. Meanwhile, beat egg white until frothy; add sugar and beat until soft peaks form. Fold in sour cream until blended. Spread on top of cake.

5. Return cake to oven; bake until topping is set, not browned, about 20 minutes. Turn off oven; let cheesecake sit for 1 hour with oven door ajar. Place cake on wire rack to cool completely.

MAKING THE TOPPING

1. Using tip of a knife, score a "ying-yang" design on top of cheesecake.

2. Place preserves in microwave-safe bowls. Microwave on HIGH until preserves are thin, about 45 seconds.

3. Spoon preserves onto each half of design. With back of a spoon, spread preserves to fill each section. ▼

4. Arrange fruit on top of cake. Chill until ready to serve. ▼

Tea Party Cake

Marzipan Mix

Marzipan is a sweet, pliable blend of almond paste, sugar and unbeaten egg whites, which can be found in tubes and plastic-wrapped logs at the supermarket. Create fanciful colors by gently kneading food coloring into the marzipan.

Pot of Flowers

To maintain the texture and design of the marzipan flowers and leaves, gently place them onto the cake frosting, trying not to press them into the cake.

**BAKING TIME
55 minutes**

GOOD IDEA Design invitations shaped like teapots and invite your guests to sample your tea party cake.

Variations

Slicing Savvy

The easiest way to slice this cake is to carefully separate the layers. Cut the bottom layer into slices first.

Child's Play

Decorate the table with a play tea set and serve these cupcakes, alongside some "iced tea," for a very special children's tea party.

You Will Need

FOR THE DECORATIONS

1 tube (7 ounces) marzipan
yellow food coloring
red food coloring
blue food coloring
green food coloring
2 tablespoons
    confectioners' sugar

FOR THE CAKE

2 packages (16 ounces
    each) pound cake mix
1½ cups water
4 large eggs
2 cans (16 ounces each)
    prepared vanilla frosting

SPECIAL AIDS

two 1½-quart ovenproof bowls
1½-inch flower- and leaf-
    shaped cookie cutters
toothpicks
6-inch wooden skewers

SERVES 16

Kitchen Tips

Create pink frosting by adding a few drops of red food coloring to 1 cup of the frosting. Add a few drops of yellow food coloring to remaining frosting; stir each until the desired color is reached.

Step by Step

MAKING THE MARZIPAN DECORATIONS

1. Divide marzipan in half. Tint half of marzipan pale yellow. Divide remaining half evenly into 4 separate pieces. Tint each piece with a different food color.

2. Shape the yellow marzipan into a rope and form the handle, lid top and spout; set aside. Sprinkle a sheet of waxed paper with confectioners' sugar. Roll out colored marzipan pieces to a ⅛-inch thickness. Using 1½-inch flower and leaf cookie cutters, cut out flowers and leaves. Dry marzipan decorations, uncovered, overnight.

BAKING THE CAKE

1. Preheat oven to 350° F. Spray two 1½-quart ovenproof bowls with vegetable cooking spray; dust lightly with flour.

2. In a medium bowl, using an electric mixer set on medium speed, beat cake mix, water and eggs until smooth. Pour batter into prepared bowls; smooth tops.

3. Bake until a toothpick inserted in each center comes out clean, about 55 minutes. Transfer bowls to wire racks; cool for 10 minutes. Turn cakes out onto racks; cool completely. Trim tops off of flat sides of cakes to make level. Reserve one top for lid.

ASSEMBLING THE CAKE

1. Spread frosting over flat top of one cake. Top with remaining cake; frost with yellow frosting. Place reserved cake piece on top of dome for lid and frost with yellow frosting. ▼

2. Use toothpicks to attach lid top; use skewers for handle and spout. ▼

3. Arrange leaves and flowers on cake. Pipe pink frosting in balls around lid and base and in flower centers. ▼

Apple Streusel Cake

Added Appeal
Fresh or dried cranberries, dark or golden raisins, fresh raspberries and even flaked coconut make delicious additions to the streusel mixture in this cake.

Dessert Idea
In addition to breakfast and coffee breaks, this moist apple cake makes a stunning dessert when served warm from the oven with a scoop of vanilla ice cream.

Icing Tip
Sprinkle the sugar glaze with cinnamon for a special touch.

**BAKING TIME
45-50 minutes**

■ **GOOD IDEA**
Substitute chopped pears for the apples. Or, for a double treat, try a combination of the two.

Variations

Apple Streusel Muffins
Alternate layers of batter and streusel mixture in a greased muffin tin, finishing with a sprinkling of streusel mixture. Shorten the baking time.

Skillet Apple Cake
A cast-iron skillet can be used to bake the cake. Watch closely while baking as cast iron absorbs and retains heat more efficiently.

You Will Need

FOR THE STREUSEL

- 1 **cup light brown sugar**
- 1 **cup chopped apples**
- 1 **cup sliced almonds, pecans or walnuts (optional)**
- ¼ **cup all-purpose flour**
- 1 **teaspoon ground cinnamon**
- 3 **tablespoons butter, melted**

FOR THE CAKE

- 2 **cups all-purpose flour**
- 1 **teaspoon baking powder**
- 1 **teaspoon baking soda**
- ½ **cup (1 stick) butter, softened**
- ½ **cup granulated sugar**
- 3 **large eggs**
- ½ **teaspoon vanilla extract**
- ⅓ **cup orange juice**

FOR THE GLAZE

- ½ **cup confectioners' sugar**
- 2½ **teaspoons orange juice**

SERVES 12

Kitchen Tips

To soften brown sugar, add an apple wedge to the container; let stand for 1-2 days. Or, microwave sugar, covered, on HIGH for 30-60 seconds. Be sure sugar does not melt.

Step by Step

MAKING THE STREUSEL

1. Preheat oven to 350°F. Grease a 9- or 10-inch tube pan. To prepare streusel, in a medium bowl, combine brown sugar, apples, almonds, flour and cinnamon. Stir in melted butter. ▼

MAKING THE CAKE

1. In a medium bowl, combine flour, baking powder and baking soda; mix well. In a large bowl, using an electric mixer set on medium speed, beat butter and sugar until light and fluffy. Add eggs, one at a time; beat well after each addition. Add vanilla.

2. Set mixer to low; alternately beat flour mixture and orange juice into egg mixture. Spoon half of batter into tube pan. Sprinkle with half of streusel. ▼

3. Spoon the remaining batter over the streusel, spreading to make an even layer. Swirl batter with a knife to create a marble pattern. ▼

4. Bake for 15 minutes. Remove cake from oven; sprinkle top with remaining streusel. Return cake to the oven; bake until a toothpick inserted in center comes out clean, about 30-35 minutes. Transfer to a wire rack; cool completely.

MAKING THE GLAZE

1. Combine confectioners' sugar and orange juice. Mix well. Turn cake out onto a serving plate; invert so streusel is on top. Drizzle glaze over cake; serve.

Attention to Detail

APPLE PRIMER

Cortland, Rome, Granny Smith and MacIntosh are all equally good for eating and baking. Avoid baking with Red Delicious apples, as they disintegrate quickly when heated. Buy firm, well-colored apples with blemish-free skin and store in the refrigerator.

Chocolate Cake Roll

Simple Switch
Turn this cake into a frozen treat by filling with ice cream. Spread softened ice cream over cake. Roll as directed and wrap well. Freeze cake, seam-side down, until firm. Slice and serve with chocolate sauce.

Easy Fill
For a sweeter cake, try jelly, canned pie fillings or pudding as a cake filler.

Fun with Fruit
Fresh berries or chopped fruit mixed into the cream filling add an elegant touch.

COOKING TIME
15 minutes

GOOD IDEA Pipe a name or a message onto the side of the cake for a personal touch.

Variations

Serving Suggestion
Place a slice of this cake over a pool of chocolate sauce. Serve with a sprig of mint and some fresh raspberries for a tasty treat.

For Chocolate Lovers
Chocolate and coffee are an unbeatable duo. Just add cooled melted chocolate and instant coffee granules to this luscious filling.

You Will Need

FOR THE CAKE

⅓ cup cake flour

⅓ cup unsweetened cocoa powder

2 tablespoons cornstarch

½ teaspoon baking soda

½ teaspoon baking powder

⅓ teaspoon salt

4 large eggs, separated

1 cup granulated sugar, divided

confectioners' sugar

FOR THE FILLING

1 container (8 ounces) frozen whipped topping, thawed

SERVES 10

Kitchen Tips

• For easier slicing, place cake in freezer 20 minutes before you're ready to serve.

• Use a large serrated knife and a gentle sawing motion to slice the cake cleanly.

Step by Step

MAKING THE CAKE

1. Preheat oven to 350°F. Line a 15- x 10-inch jelly roll pan with waxed paper. Grease and flour lined pan; tap out excess.

2. In a medium bowl, combine flour, cocoa powder, cornstarch, baking soda, baking powder and salt. Mix well. In a separate bowl, using an electric mixer set on medium speed, beat egg yolks and ¼ cup sugar until fluffy.

3. In a small bowl, using clean beaters, beat egg whites on high until foamy. Gradually add ½ cup sugar, beating until stiff, but not dry, peaks form.

4. Fold ⅓ beaten egg whites into egg yolk mixture. Alternately fold in remaining whites and flour mixture. Pour batter in pan; smooth top. Bake until a toothpick inserted in center comes out clean, about 15 minutes.

ROLLING AND FILLING THE CAKE

1. Dust a clean cloth with remaining sugar. Turn cake out onto prepared cloth; remove waxed paper. Trim the cake's edges.

2. Starting with a long side, tightly roll up cake with cloth. Transfer cake, seam-side down, to a wire rack to cool.

3. Unroll cake; remove cloth. Spread whipped topping over cake to within ½ inch of edges. Re-roll cake; place seam-side down on a plate. Dust with confectioners' sugar before serving.

Attention to Detail

Mix some mini chocolate morsels into the filling before spreading on the cake for a chocolaty surprise.

Fanciful Fruit Pizza

1 (18-oz.) roll Pillsbury®
   Refrigerated Sugar
   Cookies
1 (8-oz.) pkg. cream cheese,
   softened
1/3 cup sugar
1/2 teaspoon vanilla
1 cup fresh or canned peach
   slices, drained, cut into
   thinner slices
1 cup halved or quartered
   fresh strawberries
1 cup fresh or frozen
   blueberries
1/2 cup orange marmalade,
   heated

1. Heat oven to 350°F. Slice cookie dough as directed on package. Arrange slices in bottom of ungreased 15×10×1-inch baking pan or 14-inch pizza pan. Press dough evenly in pan, using floured fingers if necessary.

2. Bake at 350°F. for 11 to 16 minutes or until golden brown. Cool 15 minutes or until completely cooled.

3. In small bowl, combine cream cheese, sugar and vanilla; beat until fluffy. Spread mixture over cooled cookie crust. Arrange fruit over cream cheese. Spoon or brush marmalade over fruit. Refrigerate at least 1 hour before serving. Cut into squares or wedges. Store in refrigerator.

12 servings

Two-Berry Crisp with Pecan Streusel Topping

TOPPING

3/4 cup quick-cooking rolled
   oats
1/2 cup all-purpose flour
1/2 cup firmly packed brown
   sugar
1/2 cup butter or margarine, cut
   into pieces
1/4 cup chopped pecans

FILLING

1 (21-oz.) can blueberry pie
   filling
2 cups frozen unsweetened
   raspberries
3 tablespoons sugar
1 tablespoon all-purpose
   flour

1. Heat oven to 400°F. Spray 8-inch square (2-quart) glass baking dish with nonstick cooking spray. In large bowl, combine all topping ingredients except butter and pecans; mix well. With pastry blender or fork, cut in butter until crumbly. Stir in pecans.

2. In large bowl, combine all filling ingredients; mix well. Pour into sprayed baking dish. Sprinkle topping over filling.

3. Bake at 400°F. for 30 to 40 minutes or until mixture is bubbly and topping is golden brown.

6 servings

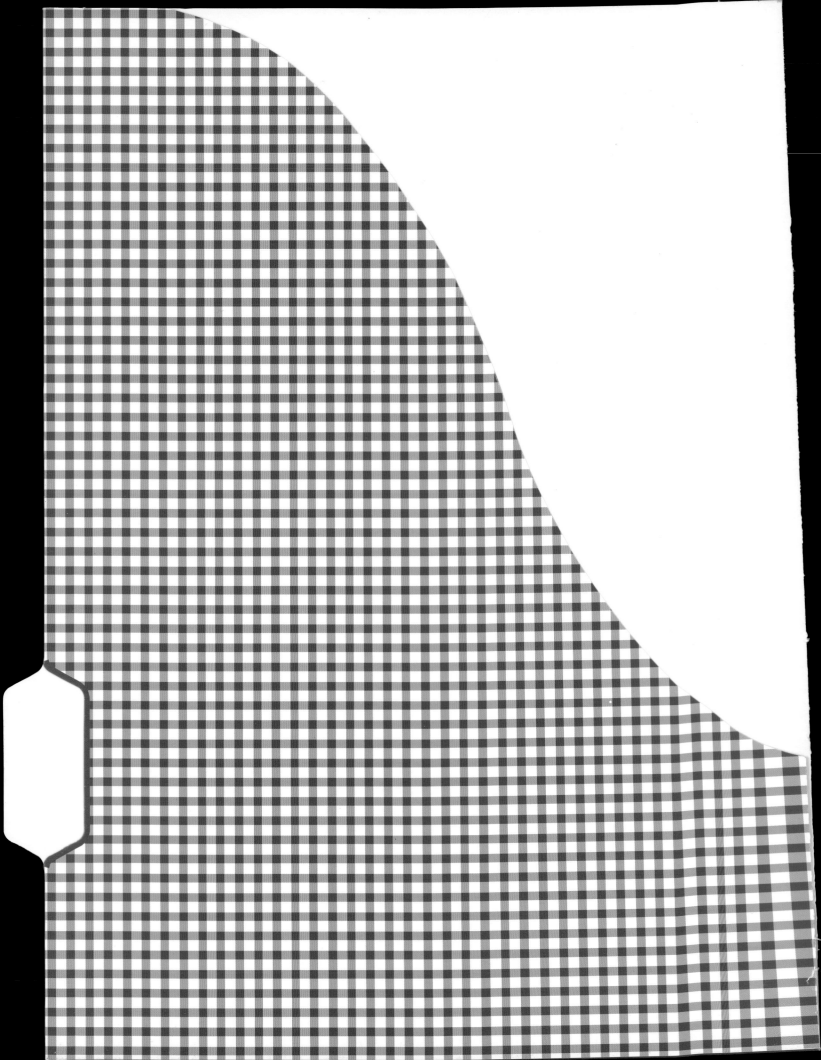